SEP   2002

GOLF.

GOLF.

Containing Practical Hints, with Rules of the Game

J. McCullough

REPRINT OF 1899 BOOK

TowleHouse Publishing
Nashville, Tennessee

TowleHouse books are distributed by National Book Network (NBN), 4720 Boston Way, Lanham, Maryland 20706.

Cataloging-in-Publication data is available.
ISBN: 1-931249-08-3

This book is a reprint of an 1899 book published by Ward, Lock & Company of London, England.

All illustrations, except those on pages 9 and 45, were created in the 1890s by A. B. Frost.

Cover design by Gore Studio, Inc.
Page design by Mike Towle

Printed in the United States of America
1 2 3 4 5 6 — 06 05 04 03 02

796.352
M

Contents

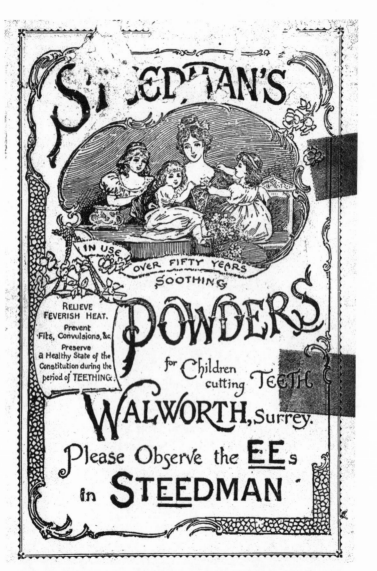

FROM

A Lecture on Cocoa

BY

DR. ANDREW WILSON, F.R.S.E., &c.

—— ⋅✦⊕✦⋅ ——

"A Cocoa Bean is a kind of **Vegetable Egg**, which contains all that is needed to **build up a living body. . . .** Cocoa is a **combination of foods**—of true foods in every sense of the term. . . . But see that you get a really good Cocoa. I should say use

PURE CONCENTRATED

which is **Ideal of Perfection.**

There is **No Better Food."**

—— ⋅✦⊕✦⋅ ——

275 Gold Medals, &c.

Never Fails.

Established
24 YEARS.

Have you a Cough?
A DOSE WILL RELIEVE IT.

Have you a Cold?
A DOSE AT BEDTIME WILL REMOVE IT.

WHEN YOU ASK FOR

Owbridge's Lung Tonic

BE SURE YOU GET IT.

Try it also for

Bronchitis, Asthma, Influenza, Whooping-Cough, Consumption.

Prepared by

W. T. OWBRIDGE, Chemist, Hull.

Sold everywhere
in bottles, at 1*s.* 1½*d.*, 2*s.* 9*d.*,
4*s.* 6*d.*, and 11*s.*

COPYRIGHT.

Publisher's Preface

THE GREAT THING ABOUT golf is that you can be an engrossed spectator one hour and an enthusiastic participant the next. Fork out enough dough and even you can traipse and play the hallowed holes of St. Andrew's or Pebble Beach in much the same manner (albeit with dissimilar results) that Jack Nicklaus, Tom Watson, and Tiger Woods do. Or, catch two hours of the Buick Classic on TV on Saturday, then hit the local muni for a quick and inspired eighteen with some buds.

Think that doesn't make golf special among sporting pursuits? Try taking your football over to Lambeau Field or your glove and ball down to Fenway Park for some fantasy jockdom, pretending you're another Bret Favre or Pedro Martinez. Guess what: It's not going to happen. But golf is different, as difficult as it can be to play. We amateur golfers can access the same equipment and many of the same venues used by the hotshots. And we keep coming back, pulled forever forward by the occasional stiffed five-iron or slam-dunked flop shot.

Another thing that gives golf a special place in our hearts is its history. The more things change, the more golf stays the same. What is past isn't necessarily passé. The equipment has changed, particularly in the last fifteen to twenty years, but the rules have remained remarkably the same as they were more than a hundred years ago. Play the ball as it lies. Don't ground your club in a hazard. Stroke plus distance. Through the fairway. Rub of the green. Casual water.

The timelessness of golf is what makes nineteenth-century writers such as J. McCullough as entertaining and informative today as they were in the 1890s, perhaps even more so. We can presume that McCullough's insightful writings about golf were not tainted or slanted by any conflict-of-interest associations with particular instructors or equipment manufacturers. A native Scotsman, he had a pedigree that shared DNA with golf's roots, and the clarity of his understanding of the game is revealed in *Golf.*, in ways both joyous and humorous. McCullough loved the game, seeing it as a welcome part of properly civilized society.

Little is known of McCullough's renown as a writer in his time. He apparently was not a prolific author of golf books, but his literary contributions are borderline magnificent, considering his profound knowledge of the game. His most fascinating work known in golf circles was his incredibly prophetic book *Golf in the Year 2000*, which offered an uncanny description of what life and golf would be like in the year 2000. It was written in 1897 and successfully portended things such as international golf telecasts, motorized golf carts, supersonic subterranean trains, and all-metal clubs. It is this level of enlightenment and feel for golf that, likewise, makes *Golf.* a handy golf guide to be treasured 103 years after its authorship.

—*Mike Towle*

GOLF.

Chapter I.
General and Introductory.

I T IS ONLY ABOUT fifteen years ago that any man travelling in England with golf clubs among his luggage was an object of no common interest and even of some suspicion to his fellow-travellers, and when they had made enquiry and ascertained the strange purpose of the leather-handled and heavy-headed sticks, they still regarded him as an amiable lunatic whose amiability was more questionable than his lunacy.

To-day—that is, fifteen years later—more golf is played than any other game.

This is a bold saying, but it is not beside the truth. It is true that more people assemble to watch a cricket match or a football match. You can sit and watch these; to watch a golf match you have to walk, which is not so good. But all these people thus assembled are spectators merely; they have no thought of taking part in the games that they

1

assemble to see—would as soon dream of going to the
North Pole with Nansen as adventuring themselves in a
football scrimmage, or of volunteering to march on
Johannesburg with Jameson as facing an over from the only
Australian Jones. They go to look on. But the people who
take an interest in golf have an active—athletic as far as
their years and muscles admit—interest in it; they all mean
to play. If a large concourse, as often happens, gathers to
watch the final of a Championship, so that the players
drive down a dense human lane, with occasional excursions
into the hedges, much to the latter's discomfort—every ill
weed or shapely tree in this human hedge is a golfer, is
watching the play not only with a spectator's interest, but
with the interest of a pupil and an imitator, studying how
he, by the great examples before him, shall improve his
own future performance. There are more golfers in the
world than players of any other out-of-door game; if any-
body doubts the truth of it I will refer him to statistics or
ask him to wait at the High Hole at St. Andrews in
September while seven couples hole out of the Short Hole
in front of him. Either method of proof is convincing—the
former is the less tedious. And not only do more men play
golf than any other game, but the men who play golf play
more golf than the men who play other games play of those
said games. For one thing the golfer golfs all the year. The

cricketer only crickets in the summer; the footballer only foots the ball in winter. But golf is always with one. And besides this there are more professional golfers than professionals of the other game—by this I do not mean the men who are paid for giving lessons and keeping small boys off the putting greens and so on—I mean men who so devote their lives to the game that it may be said of them that it has become their profession, so that when one asks with reference to one of them:

"What is so-and-so?"—meaning is he in the Church, the Stage, the Stock Exchange, or the Bar?—the answer is apt to be:

"Oh, he! He's a golfer!"

It is a sufficing life business—he is a golfer. Well, anything corresponding to this you would say about men who pursue other games, for a short time of their lives only, and for a few months only in each year.

"He is a cricketer" you could only say of a man during the few years between his schooldays and his thirtieth year, and during a few months in the summer. Even of the great "W. G." you are surprised to hear it said now and again: "He is a doctor. He has patients!" Even of the professedly professional cricketers (those who are paid, frankly and above board, for playing cricket) there are many who have another supplementary profession to fall back on in the winter of their discontent. The football player, similarly, needs a resource for the idle summer.

But the golfer is always active. The swallows come and the swallows go, but the season makes no difference to him; he does not have to emigrate—to Australia or the West Indies—for cricket in winter. He is always at it. His profession, whether it pays him or not, fills all his time. Of course, it is not the same to say that a thing is good and to say that it is popular. I am not concerned in proving the goodness of golf; I am only pointing out its popularity. But if such popularity does not prove its worth it at least seems to prove one thing, that it must be supplying one human need; and if that need be a healthy and reasonable one it comes, after all, to very much the same thing as proving that which supplies such a need to be good.

And surely the need is reasonable—the need for good air, healthy exercise, distraction from worry. All this golf supplies, and supplies it more adequately than any other game we know. Of course good exercise is not to be taken as a synonym for violent exercise. Football provides that, and, in less degree, cricket; but violent exercise is not good exercise for middle-aged men, and most men are middle-aged; for most men, therefore, the exercise of golf is better. And certainly no game will better provide immunity from worry. There is little fear of the golfer thinking about anything but his game while he is engaged in it. The trouble is rather to get him to think of anything else while he is not playing it.

And if all open air is good, no open air can be better or more open than the free breezes of the golf links—generally with a pinch of sea-salt in them. Golf proves itself equal to the supply of the reasonable need in the fullest degree.

Or you can send your undergraduate son out on the links and he will golf away, healthy and happy, out of mischief, all day long.

And equal to supplying it, too, all the life of man through—all down the seven stages. There is an age of marbles, and there is an age of "bumble-puppy" whist; but there is no age of golf—it is the game of every age. And it satisfies every age. You can put a child out into the back garden with a little club and an old ball and he will be happy and all in peace till he knocks his little sister's front teeth out with it. But then that is her fault—girls always get in the way. Or you can send your undergraduate son out on the links and he will golf away, healthy and happy, out of mischief, all day long. Or your grandfather can be given a putter and sent to amuse himself, without danger to anyone, all the afternoon on the ladies' links. No other game will serve all ends so fully.

An old man's game! That is the reproach that is most often levelled at it, with a reference to "Scotch croquet,"

Old men play it, and play it tolerably, though not as youths play it; but this only with the proviso that they learnt to play it when they were boys.

and the like. It is true that a man can play it in his old age. Is that much of a drawback to it? But the meaning of the reproach, no doubt, is that as a game it is senile, demanding none of youth's force or vigour. But of this it is only to be said that it is an untruth. Old men play it, and play it tolerably, though not as youths play it; but this only with the proviso that they learnt to play it when they were boys. Set an old man, a man of middle age, any man you please who has come to adult years, to learn golf, you will find that he produces quite a different game from that which he would have learnt as a boy—a very poor parody. He will enjoy it equally no doubt—the child of the old age is always precious—but he will not play it as well.

The history of the Championships—amateur and professional—reads us a lesson. Take the last decade or so of years—in which, alone, the Amateur Championship Tournament has existed—do we find the names of old men writ on the scroll? I do not think so. One there is, in the course of these years, who won the Amateur Championship when he was forty. None have won the open event at that age; and the majority of the winners of both have been under thirty. And that exception, in regard to the Amateur

Tournament—Mr. Leslie Balfour-Melville, namely—is so young a man, so active, strong, and muscular for his years, that he may take rank with the exceptions that help to prove the rule.

But the old man, who learns the game senily, has as much fun as any champion of them all—more. All that he does well is on the credit side, better than expectation. The champion has less pleasure in his success, a profounder grief at his aberrations. For this golf is not like cricket, tennis, football, or the rest, where the bad player amongst the good is a misery to himself and a nuisance to the world in general. At golf he does not go among the good, except with the pleasant assistance of a strong player as his partner. And even to his partner's strength he is no direct—only an indirect—source of weakness. He does not interfere with his partner's stroke or game—does not upset all balance like the weak partner in a tennis set whom the opponent will bombard with all his volleys from across the net. The feeble player at golf does not interfere with, or suffer from, the stroke of the strong.

Since England has taken up the game of Scotland she has played it with success, having champions both in the amateur and the open events. And why should she not? She confesses no inferiority in her links of Sandwich, Westward Ho!, and Hoylake to those of St. Andrews, Carnoustie, and

Prestwick, and she will not be likely to confess an inferiority in her men. Golfers had an idea, for a while, that it was impossible to play golf anywhere but beside the sea, on that quality of sandy soil that is especially known as "links." It is true that all England, and Scotland too, knew that the Club at Blackheath was the oldest in the world; but men were a little scornful of Blackheath as a golf green, one having actually ventured to suggest that the nature of the heath accounted for the tardy spread of golf in England—irreverent scoffer. But growing needs, and the ubiquitous demand for golf greens, have taught men a broader, less exclusive, wisdom. Ghosts of old golfers must be turning in their graves, with Scottish-accentuated grumbles, at the grounds sometimes used for golf by their descendants. Labour and intelligent care can make a tolerable ground for golf out of anything. The application of these qualities has made Byfleet, near Woking, a most pleasant inland course, out of a raw material of pine forest. Again, at Las Palmas, in the Grand Canary, the golfer may play golf, and enjoy it, though not a blade of grass gladden his eye. It is all on the clay. There have to be some special rules to allow you to do a little in the way of scraping away loose crumbling clay and stones lying about your ball, but with that concession it makes good practice and good fun. The putting greens, which are brown, are excellent, pounded hard with a beater so that they are quite level, with a dust of fine sand grit on them that holds the ball and invites firm putting. On no quality of soil need a man despair of playing enjoyable golf.

The qualities that make the good golfer are those that go to make the good man—with a few extra. He must have all the moral equipment of soberness, industry, control of temper, patience, firm nerve, and the rest of them that go to the composition of merely human goodness; and he will need, besides, a little private outfit of health, strength, and opportunity. The opportunity can scarcely in these days fail him, and the health and strength he may best pick up, by the way, while availing himself of his golfing opportunities. Wonderfully exact or keen eyesight, it appears, is not an essential. One of our greatest players, who has twice been champion, was rejected (mercifully) for the Navy, for indifferent eyesight. By way of compensation, perhaps, this player seems to keep his eyes fastened with peculiar steadfastness on the ball: and no doubt to look at the ball with all the eyes you have while you strike at it is of greater importance than the quality of the organs. There is a limit—it is as well not to be blind.

For the rest, whether you have these endowments or lack them, whether fortune made you for the select band of champions or the gloriously numerous throng of duffers, you will get equal enjoyment out of the game. Therefore the outcome of the whole matter is that every man should be a golfer. But what man is not?

II.

On Clubs and Balls.

W E ARE ALWAYS INCLINED to think, when we see a thing well done, that its excellence depended greatly on the tools that were used in the doing: it is a notion so much more flattering than the idea, sometimes perhaps equally accurate, that the workman was inferior to that great majority to which we belong.

And it is this disposition in human nature that is mainly responsible for the changes in the fashion of golf clubs that have taken place during such time as golf has been matter of history. We see this man or the other—Allan Robertson, long ago; young Tom Morris, later; Rolland, Vardon, or whom you will, in modern days—playing a peculiarly fine game with a club of a certain fashion, and at once the generality of the golfing world, concluding that this and no other is the fashion of club with which good golf is to be played, at once set to copy it, and play on the whole very much as they did under the previous régime.

In Our Fathers' Time.

There is no doubt we are better than our fathers in this matter—clubs and balls have improved; but they have improved chiefly by reason of the material of their manufacture, less by reason of their shape. The great master club-maker of the past was Hugh Philp. Specimens of his art have come down to us, and nothing can show greater or nicer skill than their manufacture. They are perfectly finished; they are light, very slender in the shaft, long in the head, and the faces not nearly so deep as the faces of most clubs that are made to-day. Old Philp, however, who made these perfect clubs, was scarcely our fathers' club-maker; he worked rather for the grandfathers of most of us who are of the rising generation. No matter that he who writes is of the generation already, some while ago, risen. One writes for the benefit of the generation that is rising, and the "we" is the symbol of that generation. In Philp's day golfers were few, there was but a moderate demand for clubs, and there was leisure to finish them perfectly. In the time of our fathers, that is to say about twenty years ago, the demand began to be something more than moderate, excessive—in excess of the reasonably good supply. For one thing there was no time to season the wood; club-makers had to turn out clubs as they received the wood—green; to turn out the balls as they received the gutta-percha—soft, and of indifferent quality. In Philp's time, of course, the balls were of feather, of feathers packed within a casing of leather, which, after placement, was sewn up. These balls were laborious to make and expensive to buy. Moreover, one good "top" with the iron would cut a hole in them, and the feathers would come out, as if out of a pillow: it is said that they were so closely packed within a ball that one ball's feathers would "fill a top hat."

Balls thus manufactured made golf a costly game, and few played it. It was the invention of gutta-percha, coinciding with other influences, that made golf popular. But, by all accounts, the old feather balls flew remarkably well—quite as well as the new "gutty" balls.

THE BALL FOR BEGINNERS.

But after a certain season of this green wood and this soft gutta-percha, the outcries of golfers aroused the makers at least to a sense that something better was needed. They now, at any rate, make efforts to give one seasoned wood and seasoned gutta-percha. They are not always successful, but it is something that they realise the want, and on the whole they supply it fairly—much better, at all events, than they used to. A few years ago a ball called the "Eclipse" and more familiarly the "putty"—because "putty" and "gutty" rhyme, and because the new ball was softer than the other—came on the market and did excellent service. It is on the market still, but some of its good service had the effect of running itself off the market. It had the effect of making the manufacturers of "gutty" balls attend to making them better, and with their improvement they have rather ousted the "putty" ball. Now if we were addressing ourselves to a beginner to-day we should advise him to use a "gutty" ball. The "putty" is much cheaper; it is a wonderful ball for putting with—though its nickname did not aim at the atrocious pun it might seem to imply—nevertheless it is not quite the same ball as the "gutty," does not fly with the same flight, or go off the club with the same click, and it is better to make a beginning with the ball which you are likely to use when you grow up. When it is said that the "putty" is cheaper, it must be understood to mean that it lasts better; its soft, elastic surface comes out again after being dented in, so that it does not show the effects of ill-usage. It is also a very good ball in a wind, but it is almost impossible to stop it at all dead

It had the effect of making the manufacturers of "gutty" balls attend to making them better, and with their improvement they have rather ousted the "putty" ball.

after a loft with the iron or mashie, and on the whole, after a very fair trial, it has failed to hold its own with gutta-percha.

IRON V. WOOD.

A change in the fashion of the game, that was in a measure due to the introduction of the gutta-percha ball, was the disuse of the old "baffy" spoon, for approaching. This was a club with a short stiff shaft and a very much "spooned" or laid-back face. It is rarely seen now, everyone approaching with an iron or a mashie. But in the days of feather balls, when, as has been said, a good hard "top" on the head meant destruction to the ball and a pecuniary loss of something like four shillings, it was not likely to be the habit of any man, least of all of a Scot, to use the iron when wood would answer the purpose nearly, if not quite, as well. Therefore they used the baffy; and there are a great many men who make very indifferent work, even to-day, with the iron for approaching, who would do a deal better to betake themselves to the "baffy." There is more to be done with the iron, in the hands of a man who can use it skilfully, than with the baffy. With the iron a deal more cut can be put on the ball, so that it stops deader on alighting. But to use the iron moderately well is much more difficult than to use the baffy moderately. The fatal

errors that ensue from misuse of the iron are not so likely
to attend bungling with the wood; therefore many a man,
if he would only pocket his pride, would find his game
greatly improved by the substitution of baffy for iron. The
green keeper's mouth also would be full of blessings for, on
inland greens at least, the iron in the hands of a duffer is
much more severe on the turf. It was about in the beginning of "Young Tom" Morris's career that the iron was
coming into use, superseding the baffy for approaching,
and he and David Strath, and other young professionals of
their time, brought the use of the iron to such perfection,
that, according to the law laid down at the commence-
ment, all the golfing world began to follow them, so that a
"baffy" is almost an obsolete club to-day.

There is another department of the game in which
iron has very much, though less completely, superseded
wood in the "putting." When the writer was a boy—say
twenty years or more ago—such a thing as an iron putter
was scarcely heard of. They had been invented long before,
but no one used them—for one thing "Young Tom" Morris
used a wooden putter, so all the world swore by wood. But
in a very few years a wonderful change ensued. Iron putters
became not only common but general, and to-day it is
quite the exception to see a man using a wooden putter,
though for the long running-up putts wood is certainly the

better stuff. Off wood the ball seems to go in a more springy, bouncing fashion than off the iron, which seems to keep it travelling more closely to the ground; generally there is rough ground to be passed at the start of these long putts, and with the bounding run that it gets off the wood the ball will pass over the roughness more easily and with fewer "bad kicks" than when running close to the ground off the iron.

A GOLFER'S PRESENT-DAY EQUIPMENT.

The tendency of the age has been to exchange wood for iron in golf clubs almost as much as in battleships. The old-time golfer used to carry a nicely graduated set of spoons, varying in length of shaft and gradient of face, from the long and practically perpendicular-faced driver to the short and much laid-back "baffy." There were the "grassed club"—a slightly spooned driver—the long spoon, middle spoon, and short spoon. There were also the baffy spoon and the putter, both of wood; and probably the golfer of that day would carry but a single iron club, which he would call the "sand-iron." The niblick is an invention not more than some thirty years old, and the mashie is a very much later invention again. The

The tendency of the age has been to exchange wood for iron in golf clubs almost as much as in battleships.

17

cleek was sometimes among the old golfer's stock-in-trade, but most of its functions could be performed equally well by one or another of his spoons. Compare this with the outfit of the iron-clad golfer of to-day. The latter has his driver and his brassey—this again is a new weapon, which, on its first introduction as a shortfaced club, while the drivers and so on were still of the long-faced fashion affected by Hugh Philp, used to be called, by reason of its shape, a wooden niblick, and the addition of the plate of brass to its sole was a later notion, added for the sake of protecting it when playing off roads or the like hard and stony surfaces. But, to

return to the point, the modern golfer carries driver and brassey, and more likely than not this will exhaust the account of his wooden clubs. But of irons he has a plentiful assortment. He will have cleek, driving iron, lofting iron, niblick, mashie, and, most likely, iron putter. This list by no means exhausts all the possible varieties—their name is legion. He may have a jigger, or lofting cleek, he may have a nicely graduated set of lofting mashies or approaching irons, such as even so good a player as Bernard Sayers carries. In fact, he may, if it please him, with the addition of some of the fancy sorts, such as the "Fairlie" iron, etc., bring their number and weight up to such proportions that a small pony and cart would be the fitting means for their transport rather than a merely human caddie. The advantage of such a multiplicity of clubs is very doubtful. A man must be in very constant practice to have each one of such a multitude familiar to his hand. A comparatively few well-chosen ones will suit the majority of golfers better. Of wooden clubs, as has been said, a man will need a driver and a brassey, and it is always as well to have at least one spare driver in the set you carry, in case of accidents. Then, of iron clubs, taking them in the order of their driving power, we may begin with a cleek, or "driving mashie"— the latter being merely a short-faced cleek—an iron of medium loft, which may serve equally for work through the green and for longish approaches, a lofting mashie for the shorter approaches, and an iron putter. This probably will be found an adequate and reasonable equipment capable of dealing with all the ordinary emergencies of golfing life. If a man has the good fortune to be fairly ambidextrous, it will no doubt be useful to him at a pinch to have a left-handed club. There are circumstances in which a left-handed player might get a good ball away, while a right-handed man could do next to nothing with it; and I remember a notable instance of such a case arising, in which the late Bob Kirk, the St. Andrews professional, won an important match by virtue of having a left-handed club in his set and of his ability to use it. All men, however, are not given this ability, and to the majority a left-handed club is worse than useless.

To-day the fashion is for short clubs and light clubs. Vardon won his first Championship driving long balls with short, light clubs. The theory is that with a short club you are more accurate, and that with a light club you can impart more speed of travel to the head at the moment of impact. There can be little doubt, at all events, that a long club, putting a man at a distance from the ball, must make accuracy of hitting more difficult, and the best bit of advice you can give a beginner, even before you have seen his clubs, is probably to tell him to shorten them.

Good, too, both in theory and in practice, seems to be the present fashion of short-faced clubs, which thus have their weight and substance massed behind the point on which the ball is struck. Of course, it is difficult not to believe that the fashion which we follow is the right one, yet all we who have played for twenty and thirty years must confess that we have followed many fashions, and trust we have held the same opinion about each. It is likely, therefore, that we shall follow many more before we finish, holding a like opinion about them too. Between the light and long-faced and moderately long-shafted clubs of Philp's time came an era of heavy, short-faced, and immod-

Now we are back at light clubs; we keep to the short-headed fashion, and we have reduced our shafts to shorter length than ever before. But who can say how long they will stay so, or when our clubs of to-day will take their place as fossils in the golfing museum at St. Andrews?

erately long-shafted clubs. Now we are back at light clubs; we keep to the short-headed fashion, and we have reduced our shafts to shorter length than ever before. But who can say how long they will stay so, or when our clubs of to-day will take their place as fossils in the golfing museum at St. Andrews?

III.

Elementary Hints.

CERTAINLY THE GOLFING TIRO of to-day is not likely to suffer from any dearth of instructors. His difficulty is rather liable to lie in the selection of his counsellors where there are so many, and their wisdom sometimes so various. This divergence, however, is rather more apparent than real. It could not be real because, in point of fact, the ultimate source is one—namely, St. Andrews and the swing set in fashion there by the late "Young Tom" Morris. The divergencies are in details, rather than in essentials; and even those are not many. And further there is to be deprecated a certain way, much in vogue, of testing the instructions of various counsellors. This way consists in taking a certain piece of advice—say the advice to grip tightly with the left hand and loosely with the right—and asking some noted player whether this is actually his own practice. Very likely he will say "No," and the tiro forthwith deems his teacher discredited. But it does not follow, even though the

noted professional may grip equally tight with both hands
(though in point of fact very few do; as you may see by
looking at the callosities on their hands, which are nearly
always more salient on the left hand than the right)—but
even if he does make a practice of the equal grip, his counsel to the tiro might not be on the lines of his own practice,
for he will have learned golf as a boy—almost as a baby—
while the tiro will probably be beginning some while after
he has ceased to be a boy.

To have any right understanding of the essentials of the
swing (taking the full driving swing into first and chief consideration) it is necessary to begin with certain principles,
and the first of these is that you must keep the club-head
travelling as long as you reasonably can in the direction in
which you wish the ball to go. "Reasonably," in this connection, means that the direction must be combined with reasonable speed of travel on the part of the club-head.

DISTANCE OF PLAYER FROM BALL.

The distance you should stand from the ball will naturally
be more or less determined by the length of the club. It is
the fashion of the day to use short clubs, but in any case
we may say that the ball should be at about such distance
from your left foot that if you put the heel of the club to
the ball the end of the shaft will reach to your knee when

you stand upright. Of course, when you begin seriously to address yourself to the ball, the center of the face of the club must be put to the ball, and not the heel; but in that attitude your knees will be a little bent, so that you will not find the ball too far from you.

To fix the right position further I would ask you to imagine the direction in which you wish the ball to go, and to draw an imaginary line from the ball at right angles to that direction towards yourself. That line should pass about six inches to the right of your left foot.

This fixes the position of the ball relatively to your left foot, which should point, if anything, a little outwards. The right foot will also point a little outwards, and the distance of the feet apart may be indicated by saying that from toe to toe should be about half the length of the short drivers of to-day. Relatively to the ball, the position of the right foot may be fixed as follows. Imagine a line to be drawn towards your own right, from the point of your left toes, parallel with the direction in which you wish the ball to go—the point of the right toe should be an inch or two in rear of this line.

A MUCH-DISPUTED POINT.

This, I am very well aware, is a much-disputed dictum. The relative advantages of standing with the right foot advanced and with the right foot drawn back have been discussed even ad nauseam. The majority of fine players stand with the right foot a little advanced. On the other hand, two of our very longest drivers—Rolland and Toogood—stand according to the fashion here recommended. But the fashions of the champions are not quite to the point in arguments about the best instruction for tiros. The right-foot-drawn-back position is that which is advocated in the "Badminton" book, and the writer sees no reason for withdrawing from it. For the man who is past his first youth when he takes up golf it will be found that this position enables him most easily to let his right shoulder come down and follow on the stroke.

We have now, then, got ball and two feet in their right relative positions. You are standing right to the ball, and will find that, slightly bending forward, and with knees slightly bent, you will be able to put the center of the face of the club—where the maker's name is stamped across it—opposite to the ball. In all your postures try to be easy and comfortable, not exaggerating a particular feature, not bending the knees nor stooping excessively, nor yet bracing your back and legs stiffly, as if they were jointless. Try to fall into a natural attitude. It is best to square the left elbow a little and to let the right elbow lie fairly close to the body. For the grip of the hands, the left should grasp the club more firmly than the right; and to this end it is best to hold the club well in the palm of the left hand, but rather in the fingers of the right.

THE FULL GOLFING SWING.

With the club thus held, lay its face to the ball. Then lifting the club-head an inch or two from the ground, pass it once or twice over the ball, in order to see that your muscular adjustments are in correct working order; and make the club describe in these movements a small portion of the

arc that it will describe in the actual swing. This kind of
trial trip in miniature will help you to get the direction of
the swing right when you begin it in earnest. The direction
of that swing has already been indicated by saying that the
club-head should move as far as possible along the line of
the ball's intended flight. Another way of indicating it is to
say that, throughout the swing, the club-head should be
kept at as great a distance from the body of the player as his
arms will comfortably allow. To this end it is well to keep
the arms straight as long as is reasonably possible, while the
club is being raised, and similarly, to straighten them again
as soon as possible in the course of the club's descent. For it
is obvious that there comes a point in the swing when, if
the club is to be allowed to come up, and round over the
shoulder, the arms must bend, until the right hand is close
up against, though rather above, the right shoulder. And, to
aid the swing—that is to say the progress of the club-head
over and round the shoulders—the left shoulder must be
allowed to come down and the right to come up, as the
hands rise with the upward swing, and reversely to let the
right shoulder come well down and follow on the stroke as
the club-head descends and meets the ball. The shoulders
should work as if they were two spokes of a wheel of which
the backbone is the axle. For though the shoulders go
round in this way, the backbone, between them, should

hardly change its position at all. In this manner may be effected that keeping of the eye on the ball which is one of the primary maxims of the whole business. The head is a fixed point in the whole movement; and from the moment the club is lifted from the ball, until the latter is swept away from its position, the eyes should never be taken from the ball. And if the head and upper backbone are kept still throughout the swing, there is no fear of that swaying of the body which is one of the most common faults of beginners at golf, and one of the most fatal.

Observing a fine driver you will see that as the club comes up his left heel leaves the ground and he rises, with a slight turn, on the ball and toes of that foot; similarly, that as the club comes through, after meeting the ball, he rises in the same manner on the ball and toes of the right foot. Now you should make it your study, not so much to imitate his movements of the foot, as to imitate his swing so that your feet shall almost involuntarily be lifted from the ground in the course of the swing, even as his feet seem to be lifted unconsciously. These movements should follow the swing, rather than be forced into its service.

LENGTH AND PACE OF SWING.

And this swing, of which we have now indicated roughly the direction—namely, that it should describe as large a circle or ellipse as possible—has now been spoken of with regard to its length. You, as a grown and possibly middle-aged beginner, will have taken it quite far enough back if the club comes to the horizontal behind your back. What though some young players bring it a deal further, never mind; this is good enough for you. But, after hitting the ball, in finishing out the stroke it is practically impossible that you can carry it too far. Follow through as far as you like and can: the farther the better.

The next, and final, hint is as to its pace. The up swing must be a slower swing than the down swing: this is of the essence of the whole. But because it must be relatively slower, it does not follow that it need be slow. There must be a relation, a harmony, between the two, so that all may seem parts of one whole. It should be a rhythmical performance, a kind of gradual gathering up of the great-est force or speed for the moment at which the club-head meets the ball.

It should be a rhythmical performance, a kind of gradual gathering up of the greatest force or speed for the moment at which the club-head meets the ball.

Nevertheless it is very certain that the tendency of erring human nature is to hurry the upward swing unduly: therefore the maxim of "slow up" is a good one to bear constantly in mind.

"Don't press" is another maxim of the essential wisdom of the sages, and this too has often been roughly interpreted to mean that you are not to hit hard, not to swing quick: you are to swing quickly upon the ball; the proper sense of this maxim is that you are not to hit with greater force, not to swing with greater speed, than you can control.

OTHER HINTS.

This account in the brief space allotted is as much as can be given of the full golfing swing, and contains all its chief features. It remains to speak of shorter strokes, of the brassey, the iron clubs, and the putting. Of the brassey it is enough to say that the tiro will do well if he can use it in the manner suggested for the driving stroke, and similarly in all full shots played with all clubs. It will be found well, however, as the club grows shorter, to bring the ball nearer the right foot, and to advance that foot a little to meet it, so that, in playing a full iron shot, that foot will have its toes over, rather than in rear of, that imaginary line that we have traced from the point of the left toe parallel with the intended line of flight of the ball.

It is not possible to enter into any detail regarding the methods of playing the half shots and short approaches. By way of hints it may be noticed that a shortened grip of the club will be a help to accuracy, that the hands should be brought well forward, opposite the left hip, in playing these strokes, and that the heel of the iron or mashie should be kept well down to the ground. These points borne in mind, and the left elbow rather squared towards the front, this shot, which is the most difficult, as, when accomplished, the most satisfactory of all in the golfer's repertory, should be played with fair success. At first be content with playing the stroke in a quiet, straightforward way, not allowing yourself to be seduced by the fascinations of putting cut on the ball, to make it fall dead. These subtleties will be for your study at a more advanced stage.

Thus it is to be hoped that you have reached the putting green, and in putting even more than in other parts of the game, the veriest tiro may please himself all to his position and mode of striking. Here too, as in the drive, it will be found well to study out for yourself the position, no matter what it may be, in which your putter seems most kindly to travel along the line in which you wish the ball to go. This is a problem that you may work out for yourself at home, along a line of the carpet, even better than on the links. A

At first be content with playing the stroke in a quiet, straightforward way, not allowing yourself to be seduced by the fascinations of putting cut on the ball, to make it fall dead.

firm grip with the left hand and a slight squaring of the left elbow are useful helps to accuracy here as in the longer game. For the longer putts there is but one golden rule— the ancient one—"Be up!"

IV.

On Links—Style.

T HERE IS A RECOGNISED broad division of golf links into
seaside und inland. Indeed the term "links" is only applicable in strictness to those sandy stretches by the sea on
which the grass grows so short and close that it looks as if it
had been arranged for the special purpose of giving the golfer
a well-lying ball. The seaside links, therefore, by reason of this
shortness of the grass, and also as affording those sand bunkers
which make the best of all golfing hazards, are considered to
be in a higher class than the inland links—or greens, as the
latter are better named. Men who habitually play by the sea
are accustomed to speak with some scorn of their less lucky
brethren whose fortunes compel them to enjoy the substitute
for the game on inland greens. Nevertheless some of us man-
age to enjoy our inland game very much, in their despite.
And there is this advantage of playing habitually on an
inland green, where the soil gets baked as hard as a brick by
the sun and is sloppy and covered with wormcasts in the wet,

that when you come, after such experience, to play on a real seaside course, where none of these abominable things occur, the game appears not only infinitely more delightful but infinitely more easy. It *is* more easy—the iron goes under the ball, in playing the approaches, with a kindliness it cannot show you on a baked surface; the putting green is not vexed with wormcasts; and your ball does not become coated with mud.

NATURAL QUALITIES OF GOOD LINKS.

All the first-rate seaside courses are quite obviously the result of the same natural agencies. Always they have been made by what a golfer with a little knowledge once spoke of (as) "adipose," but is better called "alluvial," deposit. They are all at the debouchment of a river into the sea, and their soil is the joint product of the river's washings down and the sea's siltings up. That is to say it is a mixture of sand and loam, with the sand in preponderance. On such soil and such formation are the links of St. Andrews, Prestwick, Carnoustie, Montrose, Nairn, and many others in Scotland. Westward Ho!, Hoylake, Sandwich, Felixstowe, Great Yarmouth, and many more in England; Portrush and Newcastle in Ireland; and if one were to give a man advice, on comparatively unknown country, how he should set about finding suitable spots for golf links, the advice would

be that he should get such a map as would shew him where the rivers debouched into the sea, and should study those spots, and those only, neglecting what was between. He would not go far amiss.

Unfortunately it is not given to all of us to have within access a links of this right royal quality. It behooves us then to make the best-shift and substitute we can. And the second best quality of ground to that of sandy links is, no doubt, Down land. Here the grass grows close and short, though not so closely and shortly as on the links. Nevertheless it will serve to give a pretty good lie. But the soil is loam or clayey—never, hardly at all, sandy. It is not in the formation that it should have much admixture of sand. Also the worms work in it, though not with the activity they display on lowland soils. Neither are the bunkers of sand. The best we can hope for is a chalk pit or quarry pit; a sand pit is of unusual occurrence, and such a blessed reminder of better things elsewhere that the golfer rejoices to be in it. Of such nature are the greens of Minchinhampton, of Stinchcombe, of Eastbourne, of Winchester, of Malvern—their name is really legion. They make good golf; but the chalky soils grow terribly greasy in wet weather.

In the neighbourhood of London most of the courses are on undeniable clay, with all its disadvantages. Nevertheless good golf is found on Wimbledon Common, on Blackheath, at Mitcham, Chorleywood, Furzedown, and other places. Curiously enough the two greens at Richmond, namely, the course of the Richmond Club in Sudbrook Park, and the course of the Mid Surrey Club in the Old Deer Park, have some of the qualities of a seaside links. The soil has a deal of sand in it, and the bunkers have actual undeniable sand. The reason of this strange

phenomenon so far inland is, no doubt, that the formation
is rather similar to that which produced the seaside links.
These two greens lie low down in the valley of the Thames,
and there can be no reasonable doubt that
the river, at some remote day, overflowed
all this low ground at high tide, and,
ebbing, would naturally leave a deposit of
sand similar to that found in the lands
formed by alluvial deposit. Even now, in
exceptional tides and floods, some of the
lower holes in the Old Deer Park are apt
to lie under water. Yet these greens do not
grow quite the same kind of short and

Yet these greens do not grow quite the same kind of short and crisp grass as we find on the true links ground by the sea.

crisp grass as we find on the true links ground by the sea.
They require a deal of mowing in the summer time, and of
course their hazards, of which elm trees form the chief part,
do not compare, for the golfer's purposes, with those of
seaside links.

ARRANGEMENTS OF LINKS.

Links, whether seaside or inland, have, of course, other
qualities and merits than those that depend on the nature
of the soil, although this is the most important consideration of all. Nature, however, is responsible for this. The
other qualities depend more on the work and artifice of

man. No green is really a good one unless its lengths are good. This does not merely mean that the total measurement of its eighteen holes should be of such and such a distance, or even that it should have eighteen holes at all. Eighteen is the number that was set in fashion by the example of our Royal and Ancient links at St. Andrews, and it has been found to suit men's convenience, one round of eighteen holes fairly filling up the interval between breakfast and luncheon, and another round taking a man well on towards the evening, and giving him a good day's exercise. But the important point is not the total distance, but the distances between the holes, or rather from tee to hole, in each case. There is a certain more or less stereotyped length of drive to which, or something like it, the majority of men attain when they have begun golf in their youth. Let us put this length of drive, with a fair run allowed, at 180 yards. One hundred eighty yards, then, is a good length for a hole, so is 360, and so is 540—longer than this you will not need them. These are good lengths, because an ordinary first-class driver should be able to reach the first in one, the second in two, and the third in three shots. This at least is the ideal at which he will aim, and it is quite a feasible one. If he plays these shots perfectly he will have a distinct advantage over an opponent who has played any one of the strokes imperfectly. But if on the other hand the holes had not been arranged in these lengths—if, for example, the second had been 270 yards, and the third 450 yards—in that case the man who had played two shots or three shots perfectly would have no advantage over the man who had played one shot at each hole imperfectly, provided he had played the other shots without a fault. Where the holes are one full drive, or multiples of a full drive, in length, there the perfect play has its perfect reward; but where the holes are at the length of a drive and a half or two drives and a half apart, there the full advantage is not given to perfect play, because a man who has played one stroke faultily but the rest well, can recover his error and so be on the green in the same number as a man who has made no mistake at all. This will show what is meant by a course of good distances.

There are other qualities and merits too. The quality of the lies through the green makes a vast difference to the quality of the golf as a whole; but this is rather dependent upon the nature of the soil than on man's arrangements—though the latter, of course, must be adapted to improving the raw material that nature has supplied. But besides this a deal depends on the good arrangement of the hazards, which should be situated so that a fairly long and straight drive from the tee shall clear them all and find a fair lie for the ball to rest on. Similarly, at the long holes, the hazards for the second and third shots should be similarly disposed. No shot should be without its hazard, for it is these that make the interest of the game; nor, again, should any hazard be too desperately difficult of negotiation, otherwise the golf will cease to be a pleasure.

And besides the hazards through the green, the disposition of those that guard the putting green is worthy of the best attention of those that have in hand the management of the course. The hazards should be arranged with due consideration to the nature of the shot by which the hole will be approached. If it is likely that the iron or mashie will be the approaching club (for, after all, it is not possible in every instance to follow out that heroic counsel of making the distances multiples of the full drive), in that case the hazard which should lie before the hole may be a great deal nearer up to the hole than if the green were to be approached by a full shot, which would be likely to pitch the ball so that it would of necessity run a deal further than off the iron, and so would overrun the hole. In a word, it should be the study of the links-scape gardener to lay out his links in such a way as to make the golf as difficult as possible, consistently with giving the reasonably well-played shot a reasonable chance of achieving success. It is the difficulty of the game that makes its interest, but the golfer is a poor human being, and must not be asked to do miracles or conjuring tricks.

ON STYLE.

Certainly some of those who address themselves to the business of playing golf adopt styles so singular and attitudes so contorted that we might well imagine them about to perform a conjuring trick at the least. No doubt there is a division to be made as broad as that between seaside and inland links, between good styles and bad; nevertheless we do see men playing golf, and playing it well, in styles so strange and various that one is sometimes inclined to think style cannot matter. The truth is that we need perhaps to rearrange our notions of what constitutes the good style and what the bad. Good style is not altogether a matter of graceful attitudes, nor is bad style expressed by exaggerated crooks of the elbow or bending of the legs. To get our definitions right and clear in this matter we must go back to the very ultimate principles of the golfing swing— must recall to mind that its essential feature was the movement of the club-head in the line of flight of the ball, combined with sufficient speed at the moment of its impact on the ball. If these conditions are fulfilled by this swing or the other, no matter whether it be "off the left leg" or "the right," no matter how singular in appearance and how

Good style is not altogether a matter of graceful attitudes, nor is bad style expressed by exaggerated crooks of the elbow or bending of the legs.

41

ungraceful to the eye of the artist the attitude in which that swing was perpetrated, it is impossible for us to say that the swing and the style are bad. And equally if we see a man in all the attitudes of Apollo, drawing his club across the ball's line of flight at the moment of impact, or checking and jerking the swing at all so that the speed is not communicated just at the right instant to the club-head, then, in spite of all the graces, we may call that style rank bad. Nothing succeeds like success, and if the style be successful in sending the ball far and in the direction wished it will not do for us to quarrel with it.

But—there is always a "but"—grace means ease and naturalness. And when we see a style that is successful, so that we are forbidden to call it bad, and yet a style that is forced, painful, lacking in grace, we may say of that style this: That though it be fairly successful in the present, while the player is young, and his muscles, though strained into unkindly postures, will obey his eye, yet when he loses the first freshness of youth he is likely to find his distorted style a handicap to him. It is, again, the old story that the well-made and well-moving horse will outlast another less well made and well moving—will continue to keep up his paces till a green old

It is, again, the old story that the well-made and well-moving horse will outlast another less well made and well moving . . .

age, because he accomplishes his work easily and without effort. The more clumsy mover may keep beside him while both are in their youth, but the clumsy fellow is wearing himself out, while the other is going easily and keeping himself fresh for his old age. It is not otherwise with the golfer: the strained and unnatural style may answer while the player is in the full vigour and suppleness of youth, but when the muscles grow stiff and the first keenness of eye leaves him, he will find himself losing his form while the more easily playing rival keeps his game for years.

V.

Match and Medal Play.

T URNING BACK THE PAGES of golf "as she was played" by
our ancestors, we are surprised to see what a large place
was held by foursomes in older golfing days. They, those
estimable men in top hats and swallow-tailed coats to whom
we owe our being, were in the habit of playing more foursomes than anything else. Perhaps they were a more sociable
folk than we, their descendants: for though we play and
enjoy an occasional foursome, we should be very far from
regarding golf so played as in any sense typical. The game as
we understand it is a game of match play—a duel—where
man is pitted single-handed against man. Foursome play we
are rather disposed to regard as a piece of by-play—a pleasant
relaxation from the real, stern business of golfing life, which
we conceive to be golf in singles. The foursomes that our
ancestors affected were not necessarily matches in
which all the players were on an equality. Rather, as it would
seem, they preferred games in which a strong player and a

moderate player were in partnership against a pair of similar relative calibre. These matches are certainly among the most interesting and enjoyable that can be played, and one may well regret that they are not more numerous. Apart from the merits intrinsic in the foursome, its popularity in the old days of golf may have arisen from the circumstance that, when golf was a more costly and less democratic game, not only did fewer people play it, but

those that did play did not devote themselves to it with the single-minded fervour of the ardent golfer of to-day. Generally, the old-time golfer was a big laird, a lord—maybe a magnate, whose local duties were a heavy tax on his time, so that he played golf as relaxation merely. Naturally he would not play it in its most finished and forcible manner, and naturally, therefore, it often pleased him to take as his partner a professional, who should help him over the hard places, retrieve his errors, point out to him their causes, and so make his day's golfing a pleasure instead of a toil. This, or something like this, we may conceive to have been a great factor in the popularity of the foursome in the days of our ancestors.

THE NEGLECT OF FOURSOME PLAY.

To find the reason of the wane of its popularity it does not need to seek far. Most golfers of to-day do a deal of their golfing by train, coming to the course by one train and leaving by another, being bound down therefore within strict limits of time. The natural consequence is that they want to get all the golf they can within those limits. In a single one gets two knocks for every one that one gets in a foursome; moreover, a single goes quicker, and is more easily got together at the starting point. All these reasons make the golfer of to-day—a quickly moving day—prefer singles. Just at the moment there seems to be an indication of a turn in the tide. Golfers appear to be waking to a notion that they have perhaps treated the foursome with undue neglect, and are beginning to revert to it a little. Certainly it is the most agreeable kind of game for a spectator to watch. There is more variety of interest, both of strictly golfing and of the human kind. One of the best known humorous positions with which golf makes us acquainted is

the position of being confidant to two partners in a foursome, both of them bewailing into your sympathetic ears
the other's misdeeds.

A further reason that has led the modern player to
abandon, in large degree, his foursome is the selfish and not
altogether satisfactory one that they do not give him equally good practice for the numerous compe-
titions which the modern golfer takes a
part in. This love of competition by score
is entirely a new feature of the game. If we
look back over the minutes of any of the
older clubs—say, the Royal Blackheath,
for instance—we find that not only were
foursomes the most common form of such
matches as seemed worthy of record, but
that the interest even in singles, as compared with the absence of interest in scoring competitions, was infinite. Virtually
there were no such competitions. No man
ever dreamed of keeping his score; it
would have seemed to him as vain a
superfluity of labour as counting the num-

*Virtually there
were no such
competitions.
No man ever
dreamed of
keeping his
score; it would
have seemed to
him as vain a
superfluity of
labour as count-
ing the number
of steps he took
between Temple
Bar and the
Mansion House.*

ber of steps he took between Temple Bar and the Mansion
House. They—these old golfers—were content to score
their matches by holes, and did not care for the decorations

of the monthly medal-monger. But they used to bet rather heavily—much more heavily than we think of betting to-day. Indeed, there is probably no game that is more free of this vice, if we are to call moderate wagering a vice, than golf. Its own intrinsic interest is found to be enough, without added incentives. It is difficult to see why the modern golfer is so fond of playing for prizes. Most of them are handicap prizes, so that no especially great glory attaches to their capture. Perhaps the desire to have a trophy to display is part of the inducement—a childish motive surely, if an innocent one. For certainly this so-called pot-hunting is innocent enough, in spite of all the hard things that some censorious critics have said of it. Men attend various meetings, and play for various prizes, it is true; but in very few cases is the value of the prizes sufficient to go an appreciable length, even when won, towards paying travelling expenses and lodging expenses. The real motive that makes men gather together, like eagles about the carcase, is an amiable and sociable one: they are glad to meet, and make matches, and talk. Being on the spot, they take the opportunity of putting in the best score they can, for the sake of the carcase; but it is altogether to mistake the reason of their gathering to suppose that any greed of lucre, as represented by the prize or medal, is a considerable factor in bringing it about. If men like to play by score, it is difficult

to see why they should not do so, or what legitimate cause
of offence they give to the golfer of the older and purely
match-playing school.

WEAKNESSES OF SCORE PLAY.

Yet to most people that men should prefer score play to
match play must seem, on reflection, an inexplicable
thing. In the first place the responsibility of score play, to
use the cant term in art, is so infinitely greater. A single
bad hole—the result, perhaps, of a single bad stroke, or
even, it may be, of a single piece of bad luck—may ruin all
the good that has been done before. So much depends,
therefore, on each stroke that to the ordinarily constituted
man, who is not a Napoleon or a Wellington, the constant
risk is oppressively great, and score play should be a hateful
thing. And half the men who start in a competition are
apt to declare, when they are half-way round, that they
will never play again in a scoring contest; but they always
do. The fashion and the spirit of emulation, and the desire
to retrieve the past, prove too strong for them; and on the
next opportunity they are at it again as eagerly as ever.
Another weakness of the scoring plan is that if the competitor does badly in the first two or three holes all the
interest in the game is gone for him. He has no chance of
recovery, and henceforth the rest of the round is a mere

procession of weariness, which he tries to relieve by affecting an interest, which is merely platonic, in his partner's fortunes.

The habit of mind needed for successfully playing competitions by score is rather different from that which is peculiarly favourable to success in match play. The former needs that a man should be peculiarly capable of playing up to his own best game, indifferent and equal-tempered alike in fair weather and foul, never succumbing to the temptation that proved fatal to Lot's wife of looking back over past errors, never allowing himself to be frightened into unseasonable and unreasonable nervousness by the excellence of his score

and consequent prospect of success. But in the match other qualities come into service. Here you are not only occupied with playing up to your own best capabilities, indifferent to your opponent, but you are on the contrary concentrating all your attention on your individual opponent, always try-ing, at every stroke, to "go one better" than him, always under the spur of his mutually emulous effort, prepared when he makes an exceptionally good stroke to do equally well, or, when he fails of his duty, to be certain of doing yours and so of getting the better of him in the end. In the match you have a hand-to-hand contest, in which the per-sonal element, the magnetism, and all those subtle qualities that go to make one man master of another, are called into active being. In score play you are going along virtually by yourself, self-centred, heeding no other's play. Both modes of competition have the defects of their qualities. On the one hand no one is likely to contest the fact that match play is the proper and original manner of playing the game whether in singles or foursomes, whereas score play is more or less of an expedient for comparing the results of the play of many individuals engaged simultaneously in playing a single round. There are only two ways, other than the scoring way, in which many players can be brought together and their execution compared—namely by tournament and by "Bogey." The tournament way is well known. The players are drawn against each other and go on, knocking one another out, until only one, the winner, is left standing. This is the method adopted in the Amateur Championship contest.

THE BAGNALL-WILD PLAN.

It is modified by application of what is sometimes known as the Bagnall-Wild plan, according to which so many blanks are added to the original entries as shall make their number a power of two—the result being that all byes occur in the first heat, and the tournament runs out smoothly to its issue ever after. This is, of course, only applicable to those tournaments in which no halved matches are permitted, but in which, as in the Amateur Championship, the players continue playing, if they are equal at the round's end, until they arrive at a decision. It is therefore better suited to those tournaments in which all start from scratch than those in which odds are given; for it is obvious that where one player is handicapped to give another one stroke in the round, this proportion cannot be maintained unless a full

The fairest plan of all is perhaps the American tournament plan, in which each player meets every other in the competition, and the winner is he whose wins show the biggest proportion to his losses.

round be played, with the result that the competition might never finish. The fairest plan of all is perhaps the American tournament plan, in which each player meets every other in the competition, and the winner is he whose wins show the biggest proportion to his losses. But this, too, requires a longer life than the ordinary golfing span. "Bogey" is a score, determined before starting, against which the players compete as if the "Bogey" were a human opponent who had done each hole in a given number. The decision as between the human golfers is determined by their relative positions with regard to the bogey, reckoned by holes at the end of the round. It is rather to be thought that the "Bogey" plan is the fairest of all those, after the American tournament, that golfing ingenuity has devised for bringing a number together in a single round. It is, in the first place, more like match play than score play, seeing that the play is by holes against the "Bogey's" score at each hole. The human element, the "moral" effect of one nature on another, is indeed inevitably absent, for there is nothing in the least moral about "Bogey." Still there does not perpetually hang over the player's head, like the sword of Damocles, that fearful "responsibility" and sense of the doom possibly attending a single ill struck ball that oppresses him in play by score. Also the "Bogey" plan is free from a most serious drawback of the tournament plan, that in the latter the good players run a chance of being drawn against each other, to their mutual destruction, while the indifferent players may slide indifferently along meeting only their own equals, so that conceivably a man may arrive in the final heat without meeting any really very formidable opponent. A modification, or combination of the scoring and tournament plans, has been tried with some success. By this method the best eight scorers in a preliminary canter, which is conducted by scoring play, decide their mutual merits by subsequent tournament play. Against

this combined method it is possible to urge that it is not just that the man who has distanced all competitors by several strokes, may be, on the score, should be called upon to start for the tournament on even terms, without any advantage derived from his previous play. All methods, therefore, it will be seen, have their demerits—the preference must be given according to individual taste. Ideally the American tournament is the best; but life is short.

Of match play there is a modification, other than that introduced by the giving of odds, namely, the play of a single man against a combination of two others, each playing his own ball, and the single man's score for each hole being counted against the lower score of either of the allied side. This is a variety that makes the game very interesting. The stronger player is always reasonably sure of having to play up at each hole, for, if one opponent fails, the other is likely to be dangerous. No stimies are allowed; and partly for this reason, partly because the interest is generally so well sustained, some of the lowest scores have been recorded by a good player playing against the better ball of two moderate players, though the match is, of course, determined by the holes won and lost.

VI.

Golfing Humours.

O NE WOULD THINK THAT the humours of golf was a topic that had been worn rather thin at this time of day, seeing that they have formed part of the theme of every scribbler that has laid his pen on the game; but happily the game, no less than human life itself, ever unfolds some new phase of humour as the years roll on, so that the clew is never likely to be all unwound. Nevertheless it is to be confessed that here, as perhaps elsewhere, the best of the new humour is apt to be unconscious.

Of this unconscious vein of humour, marked effects are to be seen in the advertisements of various country houses to be let, one and all of which are described as being adjacent to "first-class golf links." The best of these first-class golf links are generally found, upon inspection, to be of the rankly pastoral kind, and the worst generally have their sole being in the lively imagination of the house-agent, who explains his statement by showing you a paddock in which he glibly tells you "first-class links could be made." Of course, there is the alternative of supposing that he knew all the while that the links were not "first-class," and deliberately imposed upon you, but this is to suppose him a man who would never succeed in carrying that parlously named bunker at St. Andrews, beyond which lie the pleasant Elysian Fields. It is kinder to embrace the more charitable supposition that this poor man was a golfing ignoramus, whose education had been so neglected that he really knew no better; though your charity will be severely taxed if he subsequently takes you out for a game on the "first-class links" and gives you a severe beating. No properly constituted house-agent, however, would dream of doing such a thing as this; he would be most careful to let you win, whereby your opinion of the merits of the course would be naturally much increased. There is no man to whom knowledge of human nature is more valuable and more patent than to a house-agent— unless it be a golf caddie.

THE WELL-SPRING OF GOLFING HUMOUR.

The caddie himself, of course, is the well-spring of much of that humour which is as salt to our golfing life, and surely a

fine field must be open in the exploitation of the Irish caddie! Little justice has been done him yet: surely there must
be some fine tailings to be picked from him. The ore of the
Scotch caddie's humour is generally of the deep level
grade—what the Englishman calls "dry," and the
Scotchman "pawky." Irish humour is not of this quality—it
is ebullient, effervescent, on the surface. To decide which
form is the higher would be to risk a breach of international courtesy—perhaps to perpetrate yet another "injustice to
Ireland." The humour of the foreign caddie generally takes
a practical turn. The caddies of Cairo pick up your ball out
of a bad lie with a prehensile anthropoid toe and put it on
a good lie—which is ingenious, but it is not golf. At
Guernsey the little girl caddies spit on the ground, by way
of exorcism, and make the sign of the cross over the line of
your putt—that is to say, your opponent's caddie does this
over your putt, and your own caddie follows suit over the
putt of the opponent to prevent the ball going in. Faith
works wonders, but on the whole the Egyptian method is
more to be relied on. These matters, however, verge on the
serious. But either practice is to be preferred to that often
in vogue with caddies at home of putting your own ball, or
your opponent's, indifferently, into their pocket when they
think you are not looking. This is practical humour of the
worst possible taste, and expensive withal. A girl caddie,

however she might exorcise and practise magic, would never be so wicked as this.

"THEIR 'GAME.'"

There is a deal of humour, again, of the unconscious kind, in the reverent solemnity with which men of a certain golfing class—and ladies also—speak, with bated breath, of "their game." It is an undiscovered entity—value x—in many cases, but how deeply they respect it! The care with which they cherish it, wrapped in cotton wool and seclusion, declining to play with any inferior partner, "for fear they might spoil it," is very touching. Its value is evidently quite differently estimated by themselves and by others—and the most singular problem it presents is how in the world they arrived at their conception of it. On this point the author has a theory which he believes may be the true solution: They put together a series of the best strokes they ever made und call this compound "their game"—that is the glorious standard to which they nobly think they should attain; but it is misleading when they speak to others, who do not know them, of this quality of golf as "their game"—intending the term to be taken in its normal sense as implying the quality of golf that they may be reasonably reckoned to produce. Said a warrior, very angry, on a certain occasion: "It is an extraordinary thing, I've played golf now for seventeen years, and I've never yet played *my game*!"

Said a warrior, very angry, on a certain occasion: "It is an extraordinary thing, I've played golf now for seventeen years, and I've never yet played my game!"

Now, how in the world did that man arrive at what his game might be, seeing he had never played it? No one can tell; nevertheless the contemplation of that pure ideal no doubt afforded him the highest satisfaction, and did injury to no one; nay, it was rather of infinite service to his opponent, if he made his matches on the basis of "his game," as he was pleased to call it.

Golf has lately found a new home in the United
States, which has received it with all the ardour of recent
proselytes, and there we may hope to find a new and
untried field of golfing humour, for it is a humorous people,
and of a humour that differs a little from the fun of the
Irishman, the jocosity of the Englishman, and the causticity
of the Scot. Its essence is its extravagance and surprise; we
have not yet seen this quality of humour applied to golf,
and wait the event with expectation. America is as yet too
serious to be humorous over golf, except with that unconscious humour that always sticks to ultra seriousness.

"I am afraid, my dear boy," said a grave old Scottish
golfer, lately, alas! passed away, "that the game is losing its
solemnity!"

"CHAMPIONSHIP" HUMOURS.

He found the modern manner rather light, almost ribald,
for the treatment of a theme so serious; but had it not an
element of unconscious humour in itself, this mouth-filling,
tremendous "solemnity"?

Surely there is a certain element of this unconscious
humour in the urbanity with which certain people enter for
the great events of golf—the Championships and the rest
of them. To many of these, more daring than angels, the
champions could give a half, or a stroke—the latter is not

GOLF.

too big a handicap for some who competed in the earlier years of the Amateur Championship. Some of these, it is true, entered from the sportsmanlike motive of paying their entrance money for the winner's benefit—a liberal notion which entitled them to get off scot-free of laughter. The humorous point is the grim seriousness of other hopeless entrants. The Open Championship furnishes yet further illustration of the humour of some who are least conscious of it. Surely it is unkind of the Committee which has the management of that great institution to put a measure, even, of check on such aids to laughter, by enacting that none shall play on the second day of the championship whose score on the first day has been greater by more than twenty strokes than the lowest score returned. There used to be much humour, always unconscious, in the way that some of these incurables would struggle on until the end. But the action of the executive, which has put a stop to this spectacle, has been taken in the interest of the mass of competitors, and not less in the interest of the unfortunate amateur, whose kindness might have let him in for scoring for a pair of these hopeless cases. He, unfortunate man, found it very much too much of a good joke, and not at all humorous, to be dragged round the links, twice over, behind a funeral procession of this kind.

"I tell you what it is," said one of these markers once to his pair of would-be champions, "if you fellows don't play a little better than this I'll take off my coat and play the best of your balls myself"—and probably he could have done it too.

ANENT PATENTS AND PATENTEES.

Again, for a scene of unconscious humour the following incident is hardly beaten: A certain man had invented a patent club. It was not a bad patent club, and it would drive the ball as far as any other iron club known, and was quite a good weapon for the approaching and putting withal. A certain professional had holed one of the classic links in a low score with this club and none other. Therefore the inventor bethought himself of approaching this professional and buying his services to play with this club, and this only, in the Championship. It would handicap the professional's chances of a good money prize, but, on the other hand, what a splendid advertisement for the patent club, if, playing with it alone, he could take a good place on the list! It was worth the inventor's while to pay him handsomely. So, when the great day came, off went the professional, with the inventor following to see his patent work. Unfortunately the professional, in his enthusiasm for his patron's health, had toasted it rather too frequently, with a result that was disturbing to his accurate eyesight. In a word, nothing could be more pernicious than the way the poor man played, to the common distress of himself and the inventor. And the wrath of the latter, freely expressed as he went along; and gathering fury with each misdeed of the professional and the patent club, the abject misery of the performer, whom the severest taunts could only rouse to an occasional retort, made up a total of amusement for all the onlookers that could scarcely be beaten. It was an aggravation of the matter that the patentee had assembled a large clientele of his friends to see the new club work, and when it declined to work in its present hands he was fain to explain to them, in very audible accents of wrath, that the club was not having a fair trial because the wielder was "drunk"—which horrid epithet flew like an arrow barbed with the sting of truth to the ears of the wretched player, who forthwith replied fiercely that the statement was false—though he put it more shortly—and that the club was not worth a "monosyllable."

The name of such inventions is legion; it only needs to complete the list that someone should invent the much-talked-of putter, with a musical box in its head, that shall play a tune when the ball goes into the hole.

No doubt this scene was only incidentally humorous—it was not essentially a golfing humour, for the man could not be depended on to be drunk. The unconscious humour of golfing patentees, however, is another matter. Their astonishing lack of knowledge of the likely demand for their inventions is quite of the essence of the best unconscious humour, which usually depends on ignorance of some aspect or other of human nature. The name of such inventions is legion; it only needs to complete the list that someone should invent the much-talked-of putter, with a musical box in its head, that shall play a tune when the ball goes into the hole. This club we should all buy, as it would make it so unlikely that the opponent would hole his putt subsequently while the music played.

UNCONSCIOUS HUMOURISTS.

Terrible atrocities, from which a sense of humour would have preserved people, have been perpetrated in the sacred name of golf in these latter days. Watering places have advertised themselves by virtue of their golf grounds, which are generally found to be a pasture field or an unredeemed sand-drift; great golfers, even "Old Tom" Morris, are imported down to open the new course under the fearful eye of the mayor and corporation in all their robes and chains of office. It is all very well meant and public spirited, but there is a deal of humour about it too—about the ceremonial, and the health drinking, and the mutual congratulations on the opening of "our magnificent links." When the mayor in person elects to hit off the ball himself we touch a higher point of humour, but to this the civic authorities will seldom deign to lend themselves.

But ever since the round world began, the most terrible of unconscious humourists have been the children. It is, in fact, its utter unconsciousness and absence of intention that gives their humour its peculiar point. We are all aware of the fact that it is far easier to hole a putt when we have

Fore !

two for the hole than when the result depends on the single stroke; but it seldom happens to us to put the case so clearly and so crudely as a little innocent put it to her father, asking him: "Why is it, Father, that when they say you have two for the hole you always put it in in one, but when they say you have one for it you always take two?" This sort of enquiry of the *enfant terrible* is a painful method of receiving wisdom out of the mouths of babes.

Much, however, too, and again of the purely unconscious kind—but, this time, of that peculiar species that comes back, boomerang-wise, on the person of its perpetrator—is afforded by the spectacle of those who preach, on the ground of a two years' acquaintance with the royal and ancient game, sermons on its theory and execution. Especially are they insistent on this or that delicate point for decision that it is, or is not, "golf," arrogating to themselves a special knowledge and power of definition of all that this great word connotes, peculiarly edifying to those who have had enough experience to know how slight their knowledge is. But, if all this "rushing in" of certain persons, where others, more angelic, would "fear to tread," contains elements of undoubted humour, it also arouses in the spectator a pitiful feeling, not altogether making for laughter, and similar to the sentiment expressed by Dr. Johnson when he said, "Sir, these are the kind of questions that make a sensible man wish to go and hang himself." Nevertheless we are not all sensible men after the estimate of Dr. Johnson, and there are some who feel inclined, under stress of these afflictions, to "go and hang," not themselves, but these others, the foolish enquirers and the arrogant dictators. Comedy and tragedy are always very close to each other, and nowhere do we see their affinity more strongly demonstrated than on the golf green, where what is comedy to one man, the spectator, is very apt to be real tragedy to the other man, the player.

VII.

Rules and Technical Terms.

RULES.

THERE IS RATHER A tendency at the present day to regard the rules of golf as though they were like the American Constitution, "struck off at one time by the hand and purpose of man." There could not be a more radical mistake, nor one which, in a small way, has more troublesome consequences. For the truth is that so far from having been formed in this catastrophic way, they are the product of a very gradual growth, constant addition being made to them as the occasion has arisen. It therefore follows that they are not to be regarded as crystallised, and immutable, in their present form, but that we must continue to change them to suit the changing conditions of golfing life. Without this they must constantly fail to meet the ends for which they were designed; but this is so little understood that golfers of experience have now and again got up at general meetings of the Royal and Ancient Golf Club of St. Andrews, the fount of all golfing wisdom, and have solemnly proposed that no further alteration in the rules shall ever again be made. Such propositions have never been very gravely entertained, but the fact that such an idea could have entered into the mind of a fairly reasonable man shows the misconception that exists in regard to the nature of the rules.

In the first place the old Blackheath rules differed in many essential points from the rules that are in general use to-day, and in the second place the actual rules in use by the Royal and Ancient Club, now generally accepted as the law-giver, have been altered constantly as now and again seemed necessary to the golfing welfare. Within the space of comparatively few years the premier club has recognised the wish of the golfing world for a uniformity in rule, and has therefore collected into one main body such of the rules as seem of universal application, placing in a separate category under the head of "Local Bye-laws" such provisions as apply to the links of St. Andrews only. Such are rules regarding balls driven into the Eden, the "Station-master's garden," and the railway. These are separable accidents, which do not necessarily

Such propositions have never been very gravely entertained, but the fact that such an idea could have entered into the mind of a fairly reasonable man shows the misconception that exists in regard to the nature of the rules.

come in as hazards at all golf grounds, and therefore these rules are not generally needed. On the other hand, other greens have their own similar accidents of like nature, which they too can legislate for specially, under the head of local bye-laws, while using the general text of the Royal and Ancient rules.

The authority of this famous club to make laws of this general nature for the golfing world is fully though tacitly understood. No authority has been delegated to it, by any special golfing "social contract"; but it has fallen into this position of law-giver without seeking it; the honour has been forced upon it, and it has accepted it with no greedy, but even with a reluctant, hand. Lately some attempt has been made to form a body that shall hold an express, rather than a tacitly conceded, authority, to legislate for the golfing world, but it was long found impossible to conciliate all jealousies, and the state of matters remained, at the time of writing, as ever of old—St. Andrews was *de facto* legislator; *de jure*, there was none. Since the above words were written the committee spoken of has been embodied.

It needs not to go into the discussion of the rules in detail; such a discussion would be more than wearisome. But it would also be more than presumptuous to deny that on the whole they fulfil their purpose fairly well. On the other hand, it may not be amiss to point out a detail or two in which they are obviously faulty. Extraordinary as it may seem, they give no information at all as to what happens in the very conceivable case—which, one would think must often have occurred in the course of actual play—of both players losing their balls at the same hole. We are left in blank darkness in the face of this very probable contingency. Again, there is a rule that when a ball is knocked away by the other ball, the former may be replaced at the option of the owner of the ball so knocked away; but the rule does not inform us when this option is to be exercised; whether the knocked has to declare his intention before or after the next stroke played; and seeing that the next stroke has to be played by the player whose ball is further from the hole we ought to be told very definitely whether the relative distances from the hole are to be reckoned before or after replacement. Also replacement may result in stimy—or non-replacement may have that result. There is no end to the bother that this hiatus in the rules may cause. But for the defect of this rule there is an excuse; namely, that it is a very young rule, not yet arrived at years of discretion—in the sense that, by

There is no end to the bother that this hiatus in the rules may cause. But for the defect of this rule there is an excuse; namely, that it is a very young rule, not yet arrived at years of discretion . . .

reason of its novelty, its defects are only just becoming apparent. Until it was passed there was no such option of replacing a ball knocked away, therefore the time question never was raised. But men have been losing their balls presumably ever since golf began to be a game; and that no legislation should have been passed to enlighten them about their duty where both balls are lost simultaneously would be quite incredible if only it were not true. But the fact remains, beyond all dispute, so that we are able to admire the long sufferance of the golfing race, despite that it is engaged in the pursuit that, of all athletic exercises, is admittedly the most trying to the temper.

TECHNICAL TERMS.

The origin of some of the technical terms of golf is so obscure that the rules do well to make no attempt at tracing it. They do not define, they describe. The manner of playing the game is the subject of their initial description, and if the description is vague it is at least sufficient, though perhaps few are dependent on it for their knowledge of the game's nature. Even the origin of the name "golf" is shrouded in impenetrable obscurity, no less deep than that which seems to conceal the etymology of the term "cricket". In former years, before criticism was so active, we were content with the origin given in the dictionaries from a Teutonic word "kolbe," a club. That sounded good enough for most people; we were quite ready to accept the statement of philologists as to the easy transposition of "b" and "f": "k" in a Teuton mouth would sound much like "g"—and "there we were." Unhappily the subtle Mr. Andrew Lang has gone to work in his enquiring way, and has proved that "golf" has no more likeness to the old game "kolf" than it has to cricket; and hence one of the arguments in favour of this derivation receives so severe a knock on the head that it can scarcely make any show at all of coming up to time. We were the more ready to accept the Teutonic derivation, because golf is fairly proved to have been a Dutch game—though the Hollanders seem to have forgotten all about it now—by an act of a Scottish Parliament, often quoted, forbidding the importation of golf balls from Holland, apparently because it interfered with the Scottish industry. This is something like proof positive but at that time Holland was a great nation with vast sea power. It is all of a piece with her general degeneration that she should have fallen away from the practice of the great and good game. So golf remains in obscurity as to its etymology, though we may still have leanings towards the Teutonic origin, as the most plausible, although the game of "kolf" was played in a barn. Most of the technical terms in golf, however, bear a suspicious likeness to French, rather

But still, if it be only a man of straw, it may perhaps stand upright till some man of flesh is brought against it.

than Teutonic, forms. "Dormy," for instance, it is difficult, in the absence of any opposing French theory, not to connect with the sense and sound of French "dormir"—indicating that it is a condition of the game in which he who is "dormy" may allow himself to go to sleep, or that though the game is not yet "dead," in the sense of being lost, it is in that half-and-half stage between life and death—the sleeping state—in which it is impossible for him who is at a disadvantage to rouse it into active life, though by heroic measures it is possible for him to keep it going and to finish the match by a tie. This is fanciful, likely enough, and certainly the theory is one that is very liable to abuse by him who is in the state of "dormy," since according to the maxim, a match is never lost till it is won, and it behooves him to be careful that the victory is not stolen from him after all. But still, if it be only a man of straw, it may perhaps stand upright till some man of flesh is brought against it. There are so many of the old Scottish words undoubtedly borrowed from the French that their origin lends some support to the straw man, and certainly games of a nature similar to golf are played and have been played in France: *e.g.*, the present *crosse* and the ancient Franco-Flemish *chole*.

The origin of that cant term *stimie* is not too obvious, but its meaning in more general language is indicated for us by Jamieson as being "a little bit of a thing," a "small portion"—the writer has not the dictionary in question at hand for reference, but this is the sense of its meaning. *Stimie*, in the golfer's sense, evidently meant originally that one could see only a small portion of the hole, by which one could hope to enter it, on account of the intervention of the other ball. The glossary in the "Badminton" book gives "Stymie"—(sic)—though more often written with an "i" in the first syllable as the "faintest form of anything." Most of the names of the clubs tell their own tale, but there is also a tale that is told by the names of some of the clubs that have come into use of late years, so lately that very many of us can remember their introduction, and this tale is to the effect that it is a superfluity of labour to try to find too exact a definition for the names of certain things connected with golf, and

Most of the names of the clubs tell their own tale, but there is also a tale that is told by the names of some of the clubs that have come into use of late years . . .

perhaps of the cant terms used in names in general. One may instance the "mashie," commonly so spelt. It is a club that was unknown, say, to be on the safe side, twenty years ago. It is a short-headed heavy club of iron, a cross between an iron and niblick. But why was it so called? It has no etymology worthy of the term, it only acquired its baptismal name because of its weight and aspect, as if a thing that could hit a smashing, mashing blow, could make a mash of anything it hit. This is hardly worthy of being called a derivation; yet it is the way the club got its name. Another club of recent invention is a little approaching cleek, not so universally used as the mashie, but affected by some. It is called a "jigger." How it arrived at its designation is as hard to say as it is difficult to decide the etymological derivation of the mashie. Possibly it is only because its office is to make the ball jump up and loft a little way, with some suggestion of dancing a jig. At all events there is its name, and if other clubs have derived their names, and the other cant terms been baptized, on similar methods, it is clearly a waste of time to spend much philological attention on them.

Golf has spread so widely that the "local bye-laws" sometimes have to deal with peculiarities that are not met with in our temperate climate. In India we are told that the crows are so curious about golf balls that they frequently swoop down and carry them off, and in places special rules have been framed to meet cases of theft by these corvine robbers.

Rabbits are a more common pest. They do not carry off the balls, but they dig holes, even—such is their irreverence—on the very putting greens. Special rules where rabbits are inordinately numerous, are commonly framed, permitting the lifting of the ball from a rabbit scrap without penalty.

Delicate problems in natural history often, under these circumstances, occur to aggravate the already sufficiently troublesome questions strictly incidental to golf—such as whether the particular cavity in which the ball was lodging was actually made by a rabbit or by some other agency. The owner of the ball in question is generally specially insistent on the rabbitty origin of the hole, and the doubt should perhaps, as in cricket, be given in the striker's favour.

But the rule have other provinces, besides the mere execution of the game, to govern, such, for instance, as the definition of an amateur. These do not come within the covers of the book published at St. Andrews of the rules of

golf, but they have something to do with golf nevertheless.
They are made by the body that has the management of
the Amateur Championship Competition. Roughly speak-
ing, we may say that an amateur golfer is defined to be one
who does not derive an income from playing the game, or
from any direct connection with it, but that a man is not
precluded from playing golf as an amateur by the fact of
being a professional at any other branch of sport. This is
not the case in most branches of athletics—professionalism
in one is a bar to the amateur status in another. British golf

is on a different footing. On the other hand, the American Golfing Union has ruled otherwise. With them, if a man is a professional in one department of athletics, he is professional in all, golf included. Possibly there is a deal to be said on both sides of the question. In spirit one wishes to open golf as widely to all who are genuinely amateurs; but, on the other hand, it is one of the best features of golf that the evils incidental to over-professionalism are quite absent from it. It is to be hoped that it will never become a gate-money game; and in that case there is every prospect that it will escape the troubles that other sports, less fortunate in this respect, have encountered.

VIII.

Celebrated Golfers—Amateur and Professional.

I T IS SINGULAR THAT the two most famous names at present of amateurs of Scotland's national game should be names of Englishmen. It may seem an invidious thing to put two men thus by themselves, on a pinnacle apart, and one would not dare to do so by way of expression of opinion; but when one can refer fearlessly to public form to back one, it is another matter. And certainly there is enough in the public annals to show that Mr. John Ball, junior, and Mr. H. H. Hilton have at this moment the best record of any amateurs. In the first place, both of them have won the Open Championship, wresting the first honours of the game from professional keeping. And this is an exploit that no one but these two gentlemen have accomplished. Mr. Hilton, more-over, has performed the very great feat of winning it twice, his latest victory being in the year of Jubilee, on his native green of Hoylake. Mr. John Ball has won the great event but once; but that once may be said to have been an occasion of the kind that is known as epoch-making, for it was the first occasion on which an amateur had held the honour. Mr. Hilton's two wins have both been subsequent to Mr. Ball's, who is a considerably older man. Mr. Ball, however, besides this single win of the Open Championship, has won the Amateur Championship so many times that it becomes quite tiresome to have to count them. It is either four times or five—what is one among so many?—and, as no one else has been Amateur Champion more often than twice, it is evident what a fine balance he has in hand over all other amateurs. Mr. Hilton, on the other hand, though twice successful in winning the bigger glory of the Open Championship, has never, curiously enough, won the Amateur.

Nevertheless, although these two amateurs stand thus away from the rest, on public form, golf is such a curious game in its uncertainties, and those at the top of the tree are so very equal, that there would not, we imagine, be the slightest difficulty in finding Scotsmen to back an amateur in a home and home match against either of these. The man whom they would choose as their representative would almost certainly be Mr. F. G. Tait; a Lieutenant in the Black Watch. He held the Amateur Championship last year, and played remarkably well in the Open Championship this year, being beaten only by two players, of whom Mr. Hilton was

one and James Braid, the Romford professional, the other.*
A few years ago Scotland's choice would almost certainly
have fallen on Mr. J. E. Laidlay, one of those who have twice
won the Amateur Championship, and who is the hero of a
hundred fights. But for the last two years Mr. Laidlay has not
been showing up in his old form. Mr. Leslie Balfour-Melville,
a wonderfully good game player (whether at cricket, golf,
football, or whatever he puts his hand to), was Amateur
Champion two years ago, and, though he is the eldest of the
players whom we have named, by nearly a decade, would
hold his own with any one of them.

It may seem strange that in the list of those who
might be backed against Mr. Ball or Mr. Hilton we have
made no mention of Mr. Allan, the present Amateur
Champion. Mr. Allan distinguished himself, beyond all
praise, in winning this great honour in the manner he did;
but he came upon us unexpectedly. His victory was something in the nature of a surprise. Probably no element of
fortune helped him to it; but before we can give him our
confidence in matches against these tried veterans we must
see him once or twice again in the public lists.+

* N.B.—*This was written previous to the Championship of 1898.*
+ *Unhappily, Mr. Allan was taken by a sadly premature death almost
immediately after these lines were written.*

It is noteworthy that the two to whom we have accorded the highest place are both men of Hoylake, and their notable successes may be taken as a tribute to the excellent qualities of those links as a nursery of golf. It ought to be mentioned, though, in all fairness to Scotland, that both these Englishmen were demolished in the Amateur Championship of 1897 by a young Scotsman, Mr. Maxwell, who defeated Mr. Ball after a terrific struggle, but Mr. Hilton (who was markedly unfortunate) with considerable ease. Another young Scotsman, not out of his teens, Mr. Robb, of St. Andrews, played very finely, running into the final heat of the tournament. He certainly deserves a place, both by virtue of this and former achievements, among the chosen few.

It is the writer's misfortune not to be a Scotsman; therefore necessity lays upon him an exceedingly delicate duty in compelling him to note that for the last four years a Scotsman has not been champion of Scotland's national game. Almost it may be said that an Englishman has held it each year of the last four; but this would not be strictly fair to our dependencies, for

It is the writer's misfortune not to be a Scotsman; therefore necessity lays upon him an exceedingly delicate duty in compelling him to note that for the last four years a Scotsman has not been champion of Scotland's national game.

Vardon (last year's victor, and again victor in 1898) is by birth a Jerseyman. But Mr. Hilton, the holder in 1897, is, as said, a man of Hoylake; and J. H. Taylor, who won the great event twice consecutively, before Vardon, after a tie, took the honour from him, was born at Northam, in North Devon, and learned his golf on the links of Westward Ho! Yet it may be said, in justice to those that did not win, and without despoiling those that did of their glory, that just as Scotland would always back, and be justified in backing, one of her amateur sons to meet any English amateur, so she would always back, and be justified in backing, some Scottish professional to beat anyone that England might choose as her representative. As an illustration of the deceptive character of public form in this great game, it may be noticed that the choice of a representative for Scotland would very probably fall on Andrew Kirkaldy, although he has never been Open Champion. With all respect to the win-

With all respect to the winners, there is a certain element of luck in these championship competitions.

ners, there is a certain element of luck in these championship competitions. So many are so nearly equal, and there are so many uncertainties in golf, even in its highest classes, that though it is altogether impossible and inconceivable for a man to win a championship without playing a very fine game, yet it is extremely possible and conceivable for many others in the competition to be equally fine players and yet not to win. Every man has his days—good days and bad days—at golf, the fine player like (though his variability does not run over so wide a scale) an indifferent player. The championships occupy but few days in the year, and out of a large field of players approximately equal the honour is to him whose "day" coincides with the championship dates.

An upholder of Scotland's honour, even more powerful, perhaps, than Andrew Kirkaldy, might be found in A. Herd. We have rather forgotten to rank Herd amongst the Scotsmen, so long has he been resident at Huddersfield, in the employ of the local club; but it is certain that there is no finer nor more consistent golfer in the kingdom. Yet he, singularly enough, even as Kirkaldy, has not won a championship. Competitions of equal importance, in respect of the entry list, he has won in plenty, but the championship he has always just failed to win. It has not happened to be his day. The general golfing opinion is very just in this particular. It does not allow its verdict to be guided exclusively by championship

Competitions of equal importance, in respect of the entry list, he has won in plenty, but the championship he has always just failed to win. It has not happened to be his day.

results, and is able to recognise the tremendous strength of some who have not been champions even as superior to that of one or two who have. H. Vardon, last year's Champion, has a brother, Tom Vardon, who is very nearly an equally fine player, and beat his Champion brother not long ago in an exhibition match on a neutral green. Both learned their golf on the excellent links of Jersey, and both are now resident in England, where, both personally and by virtue of their golfing powers, they have made multitudes of friends. A remarkably easy style is that of Harry Vardon, the ex-Champion. Like Mr. Hilton, the Champion of 1897, he looks as if the game were no trouble to him, and he has the excellent gift of an even temper in prosperity and adversity alike. James Braid, of Romford, who was within a stroke of Mr. Hilton at Hoylake, in 1897, has an advantage over most mortals in his strength and resultant length of swing. He, too, is gifted with the most equable disposition, to his advantage both as man and golfer. But for a little loose play, the result no doubt of a slight natural nervousness, at the sixteenth and seventeenth holes of his last round, he would even have been below Mr. Hilton's winning score.

The name of the first-class professionals is legion. It is in their numbers that they have the advantage of the amateurs. In the latter class there are generally half a dozen or so that might possibly be backed on level terms against the pick of the professionals—though the latter would probably have the advantage; but if it came to a team match of some twenty aside, the balance in the professionals' favour would be infinitely heavier. To name but a few of their leaders: there is Willie Fernie, of Troon, who has delivered lectures on the golfing swing; and Willie Park, who has written a book on the game, and is to play a great match with Vardon in July 1899. Willie Dunn has started a gymnasium, where he gives practical instruction and exercises, but this is in New York, where golf is pursued with all the fury of the new convert. There is Sayers, at North Berwick, where he seems to break his own record every other day; David Grant, his brother-in-law, is a fine player, too, of a less ambitious order. There is Jack White, at the Seaford Club, in Sussex. There is David Brown, ex-Champion, at Malvern, on the course of the Worcestershire Club. There is Archie Simpson, at Aberdeen; Willie Auchterlonie, ex-Champion, at St. Andrews; young Kinnell, lately at Leven, and now gone to Prestwick; and there is "Old Tom" Morris, now, as always, at St. Andrews, the Nestor of them all.

There are a multitude more whose names we can only pass over in an apologetic silence: and as many as are the men, so many are the styles. Perhaps it is not too much to say that amongst them all the ideal of style is not to be found—only examples of different points of perfection. It would need a composite creation to embody them all. But if one had to make a choice, and pick out the finest style of any, combining the utmost power with the utmost grace—one would be less inclined to search for it among the professional than in the amateur ranks, and the suffrages of many would put Mr. Ball on the pedestal. At the same time grace is not always the sign of power. There have been one or two examples, within recent golfing experience, of beautiful styles that have altogether failed to achieve their ends; and there are instances without number of singularly ungraceful styles proving wonderful-

There have been one or two examples, within recent golfing experience, of beautiful styles that have altogether failed to achieve their ends; and there are instances without number of singularly ungraceful styles proving wonderfully effective.

ly effective. It is probable that by degrees we shall arrive at greater uniformity of style than prevails at present. Golfers, in course of the recent spread of the game into corners of the earth where it was before unknown, have been in the habit of forming styles of their own, evolving the game out of their inner consciousness, or from what they had learned from such games as cricket. And this produced some singular results when applied to golf. But new instructors, who either learned the game at St. Andrews, or whose knowledge is derived from that great elemental source, are on practically every green, so that no barbarians of the south have an excuse for failing to adopt the classical style.

Probably it would be generally conceded, whatever view we may take of the style of modern players as compared with that of an older school, that execution has generally improved. But, however that may be, it is almost certain that relatively the play of amateur golfers in general is much better than in the older days. Until some ten or fifteen years ago it was a very rare thing for amateurs to take any part in the Open Championship; and the notion that it could be won by any of them was regarded as quite chimerical. Now, as we have noted, an amateur has won it thrice, and one amateur has won it twice off his own bat, or club. The professional and amateur classes have thus been brought closer together. Maybe the latter give more time to it than they did a decade ago.

The victory of one amateur, Mr. Ball, made it more likely that the victory would be repeated. It gave those who came after a better hope, and dispelled the nervousness that is likely to assail all but the least susceptible to such influences on finding an unprecedentedly great feat on the eve of accomplishment at their hands.

There are one or two amateurs who probably play as much golf as most of the professionals. Some of the latter have much of their time occupied with club making, but even this is not altogether wasted time, even from the strict golf-playing point of view; for the constant handling of the clubs that goes on in the shops is a means in itself of making the "feel" of the club familiar, and undoubtedly the power he has of making and altering his clubs exactly to his own fancy is a great point in the club-maker's favour. There are one or two amateurs who are able to make and mend as well as the best professors of the art, and they have their reward. A boy, learning golf as an amateur, would do well to pick up what smattering he can of the club-making mystery. It will serve him well in his golfing life, beside saving club-makers' bills.

IX.

Rules of the Game of Golf by the Royal and Ancient Golf Club of St. Andrews.

1. THE GAME OF GOLF is played by two or more sides, each playing its own ball. A side may consist of one or more persons.

2. The game consists in each side playing a ball from a tee into a hole by successive strokes, and the hole is won by the side holing its ball in the fewest strokes, except as otherwise provided for in the Rules. If two sides hole out in the same number of strokes, the hole is halved.

3. The teeing ground shall be indicated by two marks placed in a line at right angles to the course, and the player shall not tee in front of, nor on either side of, these marks, nor more than two club lengths behind

them. A ball played from outside the limits of the tee-ing ground, as thus defined, may be recalled by the opposite side. The hole shall be forty-three inches in diameter, and at least four inches deep.

4. The ball must be fairly struck at, and not pushed, scraped, or spooned under penalty of the loss of the hole. Any movement of the club which is intended to strike the ball is a stroke.

5. The game commences by each side playing a ball from the first teeing ground. In a match with two or more on a side, the partners shall strike off alternate-ly from the tees, and shall strike alternately during the play of the hole. The players who are to strike against each other shall be named at starting, and shall continue in the same order during the match. The player who shall play first on each side shall be named by his own side. In case of failure to agree, it shall be settled by lot or toss which side shall have the option of leading.

6. If a player shall play when his partner should have done so, his side shall lose the hole, except in the case of the tee shot, when the stroke may be recalled at the option of the opponents.

7. The side winning a hole shall lead in starting for the next hole, and may recall the opponent's strokes

should he play out of order. This privilege is called the "honour." On starting for a new match, the winner of the long match in the previous round is entitled to the "honour." Should the first match have been halved, the winner of the last hole gained is entitled to the "honour."

8. One round of the Links—generally eighteen holes—is a match, unless otherwise agreed upon. The match is won by the side which gets more holes ahead than there remain holes to be played, or by the side winning the last hole when the match was all even at the second last hole. If both sides have won the same number it is a halved match.

9. After the balls are struck from the tee, the ball furthest from the hole to which the parties are playing shall be played first, except as otherwise provided for in the Rules. Should the wrong side play first, the opponent may recall the stroke before his side has played.

10. Unless with the opponent's consent, a ball struck from the tee shall not be changed, touched, or moved before the hole is played out, under the penalty of one stroke, except as otherwise provided for in the Rules.

11. In playing through the green, all loose impediments within a club length of a ball which is not lying in or touching a hazard, may be removed, but loose

impediments which are more than a club length from the ball shall not be removed under the penalty of one stroke.

12. Before striking at the ball, the player shall not move, bend, or break anything fixed or growing near the ball, except in the act of placing his feet on the ground for the purpose of addressing the ball, and in soling his club to address the ball, under the penalty of the loss of the hole, except as provided for in Rule 18.

13. A ball stuck fast in wet ground or sand may be taken out and replaced loosely in the hole which it has made.

14. When a ball lies in or touches a hazard, the club shall not touch the ground, nor shall anything be touched or moved before the player strikes at the ball, except that the player may place his feet firmly on the ground for the purpose of addressing the ball, under the penalty of the loss of the hole.

15. A "hazard" shall be any bunker of whatever nature— water, sand, loose earth, mole hills, paths, roads, or railway, whin bushes, rushes, rabbit scrapes, fences, ditches, or anything which is not the ordinary green of the course, except sand blown on to the grass by wind, or sprinkled on grass for the preservation of the Links, or snow or ice, or bare patches on the course.

16. A player or a player's caddie shall not press down or remove any irregularities of surface near the ball,

except at the Teeing Ground, under the penalty of the loss of the hole.

17. If any vessel, wheelbarrow, tool, roller, grass-cutter, box, or other similar obstruction has been placed upon the course, such obstruction may be removed. A ball lying on or touching such obstruction, or on clothes, or nets, or on ground under repair, or temporarily covered up or opened, may be lifted and dropped at the nearest point of the course; but a ball lifted in a hazard shall be dropped in the hazard. A ball lying in a golf hole or flag hole may be lifted and dropped not more than a club length behind such hole.

18. When a ball is completely covered with fog, bent, whins, etc., only so much thereof shall be set aside as that the player shall have a view of his ball before he plays, whether in a line with the hole or otherwise.

19. When a ball is to be dropped, the player shall drop it. He shall front the hole, stand erect behind the hazard, keep the spot from which the ball was lifted (or in the case of running water, the spot at which it entered) in a line between him and the hole, and drop the ball behind him from his head, standing as far behind the hazard as he may please.

20. When the balls in play lie within six inches of each other—measured from their nearest points—the ball

nearer the hole shall be lifted until the other is played, and shall then be replaced as nearly as possible in its original position. Should the ball further from the hole be accidentally moved in so doing, it shall be replaced. Should the lie of the lifted ball be altered by the opponent in playing, it may be placed in a lie near to, and as nearly as possible similar to that from which it was lifted.

21. If a ball lie or be lost in water, the player may drop a ball under the penalty of one stroke.

22. Whatever happens by accident to a ball in motion, such as its being deflected or stopped by any agency outside the match, or by the forecaddie, is a "rub of the green," and the ball shall be played from where it lies. Should a ball lodge in anything moving, such ball, or if it cannot be recovered, another ball, shall be dropped as nearly as possible at the spot where the object was when the ball lodged in it. But if a ball at rest be displaced by any agency outside the match, the player shall drop it or another ball as nearly as possible at the spot where it lay. On the Putting Green the ball may be replaced by hand.

23. If the player's ball strike, or be accidentally moved by an opponent or an opponent's caddie or clubs, the opponent loses the hole.

24. If the player's ball strike, or be stopped by himself or his partner, or either of their caddies or clubs, or if, while in the act of playing, the player strike the ball twice, his side loses the hole.

25. If the player when not making a stroke, or his partner, or either of their caddies, touch their side's ball, except at the tee, so as to move it, or by touching anything cause it to move, the penalty is one stroke.

26. A ball is considered to have been moved if it leave its original position in the least degree and stop in another; but if a player touch his ball and thereby cause it to oscillate, without causing it to leave its original position, it is not moved in the sense of Rule 25.

27. A player's side loses a stroke if he play the opponent's ball, unless (1) the opponent then play the player's ball, whereby the penalty is cancelled, and the hole must be played out with the balls thus exchanged, or (2) the mistake occur through wrong information given by the opponent, in which case the mistake, if discovered before the opponent has played, must be rectified by placing a ball as nearly as possible where the opponent's ball lay. If it be discovered before either side has struck off at the tee that one side has played out the previous hole with the ball of a party not engaged in the match, that side loses that hole.

28. If a ball be lost, the player's side loses the hole. A ball shall be held as lost if it be not found within five minutes after the search is begun.

29. A ball must be played wherever it lies, or the hole be given up, except as otherwise provided for in the Rules.

30. The term "Putting Green" shall mean the ground within twenty yards of the hole, excepting hazards.

31. All loose impediments may be removed from the Putting Green, except the opponent's ball when at a greater distance from the player's than six inches.

32. In a match of three or more sides, a ball in any degree lying between the player and the hole must be lifted, or if on the Putting Green holed out.

33. When the ball is on the Putting Green, no mark shall be placed, nor line drawn as a guide. The line to the hole may be pointed out, but the person doing so may not touch the ground with the hand or club. The player may have his own or his partner's caddie to stand at the hole, but none of the players or their caddies may move, so as to shield the ball from, or expose it to, the wind. The penalty for any breach of this rule is the loss of the hole.

34. The player or his caddie may remove (but not press down) sand, earth, wormcasts, or snow lying around

the hole or on the line of his putt. This shall be done by brushing lightly with the hand only across the putt and not along it. Dung may be removed to a side by an iron club, but the club must not be laid with more than its own weight upon the ground. The putting line must not be touched by club, hand, or foot, except as above authorized, or immediately in front of the ball in the act of addressing it, under the penalty of the loss of the hole.

35. Either side is entitled to have the flag-stick removed when approaching the hole. If the ball rest against the flag-stick when in the hole, the player shall be entitled to remove the stick, and if the ball fall in it shall be considered as holed out in the previous stroke.

36. A player shall not play until the opponent's ball shall have ceased to roll, under the penalty of one stroke. Should the player's ball knock in the opponent's ball, the latter shall be counted as holed out in the previous stroke. If, in playing, the player's ball displace the opponent's ball, the opponent shall have the option of replacing it.

37. A player shall not ask for advice, nor be knowingly advised about the game by word, look, or gesture from anyone except his own caddie, or his partner's caddie, under the penalty of the loss of the hole.

GOLF.

38. If a ball splits into several pieces, another ball may be put down where the largest portion lies, or if two pieces are apparently of equal size, it may be put where either piece lies, at the option of the player. If a ball crack or become unplayable, the player may change it, on intimating to his opponent his intention to do so.

39. A penalty stroke shall not be counted the stroke of a player, and shall not affect the rotation of play.

40. Should any dispute arise on any point, the players have the right of determining the party or parties to whom the dispute shall be referred, but should they not agree, either party may refer it to the Green Committee of the Green where the dispute occurs, and their decision shall be final. Should the dispute not be covered by the Rules of Golf, the arbiters must decide it by equity.

SPECIAL RULES FOR MEDAL PLAY.

1. In Club competitions, the competitor doing the stipulated courses in fewer strokes shall be the winner.

2. If the lowest score be made by two or more competitors, the ties shall be decided by another round, to be played either on the same or on any other day as the Captain, or in his absence, the Secretary, shall direct.

3. New holes shall be made for the Medal round, and thereafter no member shall play any stroke on a Putting Green before competing.

4. The scores shall be kept by a special marker, or by the competitors noting each other's scores. The scores marked shall be checked at the finish of each hole. On completion of the course, the score of the player shall be signed by the person keeping the score, and handed to the Secretary.

5. If a ball be lost, the player shall return as nearly as possible to the spot where the ball was struck, tee another ball, and lose a stroke. If the lost ball be found before he has struck the other ball, the first shall continue in play.

6. If the player's ball strike himself, or his clubs or caddie, or if in the act of playing, the player strike the ball twice, the penalty shall be one stroke.

7. If a competitor's ball strike the other player or his clubs or caddie, it is a "rub of the green," and the ball shall be played from where it lies.

8. A ball may, under the penalty of two strokes, be lifted out of a difficulty of any description, and be teed behind same.

9. All balls shall be holed out, and when play is on the Putting Green, the flag shall be removed, and the

GOLF.

competitor whose ball is nearest the hole shall have the option of holing out first, or of lifting his ball, if it be in such a position that it might, if left, give an advantage to the other competitor. Throughout the green a competitor can have the other competitor's ball lifted, if he finds that it interferes with his stroke.

10. A competitor may not play with a professional, and he may not receive advice from anyone but his caddie. A forecaddie may be employed.

11. Competitors may not discontinue play because of bad weather.

12. The penalty for a breach of any Rule shall be disqualification.

13. Any dispute regarding the play shall be determined by the Green Committee.

14. The ordinary Rules of Golf, so far as they are not at variance with these special rules, shall apply to medal play.

LOCAL RULES FOR ST. ANDREWS LINKS.

1. When the Green Committee consider it necessary a Telegraph Board shall be used to give the numbers for starting.

2. If the ball lie in any position in the Swilcan Burn, whether in water or not, the player may drop it, or if it cannot be recovered, another ball may be dropped on the line where it entered the burn on the opposite side to the hole to that to which he is playing under the penalty of one stroke.

3. Should a ball be driven into the water of the Eden at the high hole, or into the sea at the first hole, the ball, or, if it cannot be recovered, another ball, shall be teed a club length in front of either river or sea

near the spot where it entered, under the penalty of one stroke.

4. A ball in the enclosure (between road and dyke holes) called the Station Master's Garden, shall be a lost ball.

5. If a ball lie within two yards of a fixed seat, it may be lifted and dropped two yards to the side of the seat farthest from the hole.

6. Any dispute respecting the play shall be determined by the Green Committee.

7. Competitors for the Spring and Autumn Medals of the Club (with the exception of the George Glennie Medal, shall be decided by playing one round of the Links, and the competitor doing it in fewest strokes shall be the winner.

8. The order of starting for the Spring and Autumn Medals will be ballotted for on the previous evening, and intending Competitors must give in their names to the Secretary not later than Five o'clock on the previous evening. Any competitor not at the Teeing Ground when his number is called shall be disqualified, unless it be proved to the satis- faction of the Green Committee or Secretary that he has a valid excuse, such as serious temporary ill- ness, a train late or such like, in which case he may

be allowed to compete and if allowed, shall be placed at the bottom of the list. The absent competitor's partner may start in his proper turn, provided he get another player to play with him.

9. Competitors for medals or prizes are not allowed to delay starting on account of bad weather, but must strike off immediately after the preceding party has crossed the burn, and, after they have started, are not allowed to take shelter, but must complete their round in the order of their start. In cases of stoppage by accident, or severe temporary illness, the Green Committee may allow a competitor to resume play.

10. All private matches must be delayed till the last medal competitors have holed out at the first hole.

THE ESTABLISHED ETIQUETTE OF GOLF.

No player, caddie, or onlooker should move or talk during a stroke.

No player should play from the tee until the party in front have played their second strokes and are out of range, nor play to the Putting Green till the party in front have holed out and moved away.

The player who leads from the tee should be allowed to play before his opponent tees his ball.

Players who have holed out should not try their putts over again when other players are following them.

Players looking for a lost ball must allow any other match coming up to pass them.

A party playing three or more balls must allow a two-ball match to pass them.

A party playing a shorter round must allow a two-ball match playing the whole round to pass them.

A player should not putt at the hole when the flag is in it.

The reckoning of the strokes is kept by the terms "the odd," "two more," "three more," etc., and "one off three," "one off two," "the like." The reckoning of the strokes is kept by the terms—so many "holes up"—or "all even"—and—so many "to play."

Turf cut or displaced by a stroke in playing should be at once replaced.